RISE UP AND FIGHT

VOLUME ONE

APOSTLE GARY M. DUNN

EDITED BY
NICOLE QUEEN

VISION PUBLISHING
HOUSE

Vision Publishing House
www.vision-publishinghouse.com

ISBN: 978-1-955297-59-2

To every warrior who knows it's time to fight—
Put on your armor, pick up your sword, and let's fight…
The time is now!

For you equipped me with strength for the battle.

PSALM 18:39

CONTENTS

INTRODUCTION

Welcome to *Rise Up And Fight*, the first volume of a transformative three-part series designed to guide you through a 30-day journey of spiritual empowerment and renewal. This devotional series is a call to arms for those seeking to deepen their relationship with God, to discover their inner strength, and to engage in the daily battle for faith with renewed vigor and determination.

This journey is structured to provide you with a comprehensive spiritual toolkit, enabling you to face life's challenges with the wisdom and power of God's Word at your side. Each day unfolds a new facet of spiritual illumination, unveiling profound truths that resonate across time and circumstance. The verses drawn from the Bible are life-giving streams of wisdom. They are a pilgrimage through the realms of faith, courage, and the boundless love of Almighty God.

As you delve into the pages that follow, may you find solace, inspiration, and a divine compass for the days yet to come. May your reflections be a testament to the enduring power of faith and the unyielding love of the Creator.

HOW TO USE THIS BOOK

This book is organized into 30 days. Each day consists of the following:

- **Scripture Reading**: This is given to highlight a facet of God's truth for your daily focus.

- **Power Principle**: This insightful statement captures the essence of your Scripture Reading, as a beacon of light directing your focus throughout the day.

- **Prophetic Prayer**: This prayer, grounded in Scripture, will guide you into the comforting presence of God.

- **Preparation for War**: In this journaling space, you're invited to engage in meaningful moments of meditation with God, to reflect on your strategy, next steps, and prayer response.

- **Scripture Writing & Reflection**: On the additional lines, you can rewrite your daily Scripture Reading several times to help you commit it to memory. You can also record any additional insight or revelation from God.

DAY 1: CRY OUT FOR DELIVERANCE

 And Israel was greatly impoverished because of the Midianites; and the children of Israel cried unto the Lord.

JUDGES 6:5

POWER PRINCIPLE

God hears the cries of His people and delivers them from their afflictions.

PROPHETIC PRAYER

Heavenly Father, in times of trouble and oppression, we turn to You for deliverance and guidance. Just as the children of Israel cried out to You in their distress, we lift our voices to You today. Hear our prayers, O Lord, and come to our aid. Deliver us from our troubles and grant us strength and courage to face the challenges before us. We trust in Your faithfulness and love. In Jesus' Name, Amen.

PREPARATION FOR WAR

What strategy has God revealed to you after reading today's message?

_____

_____

_____

_____

_____

What are the next steps you need to take?

_____

_____

_____

_____

_____

Journal your prayer to God in response to His Word.

_____

_____

_____

_____

_____

SCRIPTURE WRITING & REFLECTION

_____

_____

_____

_____

_____

_____

_____

_____

DAY 2: RECEIVE DIVINE REVELATION

 Surely the Lord God will do nothing, but he revealeth his secret unto his servants the prophets.

AMOS 3:7 KJV

POWER PRINCIPLE

God communicates His plans through His chosen messengers.

PROPHETIC PRAYER

Heavenly Father, thank You for revealing Your divine will through Your prophets. As I seek Your daily guidance, help me be attentive to Your voice and the messages You send through Your servants. Grant me wisdom and discernment to understand Your revelations and align my life with Your purposes. In Jesus' Name, Amen.

PREPARATION FOR WAR

What strategy has God revealed to you after reading today's message?

_____

_____

_____

_____

_____

What are the next steps you need to take?

_____

_____

_____

_____

Journal your prayer to God in response to His Word.

_____

_____

_____

_____

SCRIPTURE WRITING & REFLECTION

_____

_____

_____

_____

_____

_____

_____

DAY 3: BELIEVE IN GOD AND HIS PROPHETS

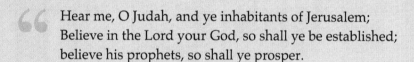

> Hear me, O Judah, and ye inhabitants of Jerusalem; Believe in the Lord your God, so shall ye be established; believe his prophets, so shall ye prosper.
>
> 2 CHRONICLES 20:20

POWER PRINCIPLE

Faith in God and His messengers leads to establishment and prosperity.

PROPHETIC PRAYER

Heavenly Father, I acknowledge my faith in You and Your prophets. Just as Jehoshaphat encouraged the people to believe, I pray for unwavering faith in Your promises and the messages delivered by Your chosen messengers. Strengthen my trust in Your guidance, that I may be firmly established and prosper in all aspects of my life. In Jesus' Name, Amen.

PREPARATION FOR WAR

What strategy has God revealed to you after reading today's message?

_____

_____

_____

_____

_____

What are the next steps you need to take?

_____

_____

_____

_____

Journal your prayer to God in response to His Word.

_____

_____

_____

_____

_____

SCRIPTURE WRITING & REFLECTION

_____

_____

_____

_____

_____

_____

_____

_____

DAY 4: REVERE THE PRESENCE OF GOD

 Tremble, thou earth, at the presence of the Lord, at the presence of the God of Jacob.

PSALM 114:7

POWER PRINCIPLE

In the presence of God, all creation trembles and stands in awe.

PROPHETIC PRAYER

Mighty God, Creator of the heavens and the earth, Your presence is humbling. As we meditate on Your Word, we acknowledge that even the earth trembles at the mention of Your name. Help us to approach Your presence with reverence and gratitude, understanding the magnitude of who You are. May we be filled with awe at Your greatness, and may our lives reflect our reverence for You. In Jesus' Name, Amen.

PREPARATION FOR WAR

What strategy has God revealed to you after reading today's message?

_____

_____

_____

_____

_____

What are the next steps you need to take?

_____

_____

_____

_____

_____

Journal your prayer to God in response to His Word.

_____

_____

_____

_____

_____

SCRIPTURE WRITING & REFLECTION

_____

_____

_____

_____

_____

_____

_____

_____

_____

DAY 5: GOD IS OUR DELIVERER AND PROVIDER

 And I delivered you out of the hand of the Egyptians, and out of the hand of all that oppressed you, and drave them out from before you, and gave you their land.

JUDGES 6:9

POWER PRINCIPLE

God is faithful to deliver His people from oppression and provide for their needs.

PROPHETIC PRAYER

Heavenly Father, we praise You for being our Deliverer and Provider, just as You delivered the Israelites from the hand of the Egyptians and their oppressors. You are faithful to fulfill Your promises and lead us to the land of abundance. We thank You for Your unending grace and mercy in our lives. Help us to trust in Your provision and guidance each day, knowing that You are always with us, leading us into the fullness of Your promises. In Jesus' Name, Amen.

PREPARATION FOR WAR

What strategy has God revealed to you after reading today's message?

_____

_____

_____

_____

_____

What are the next steps you need to take?

_____

_____

_____

_____

_____

Journal your prayer to God in response to His Word.

_____

_____

_____

_____

_____

SCRIPTURE WRITING & REFLECTION

_____

_____

_____

_____

_____

_____

_____

_____

DAY 6: FIGHT THE GOOD FIGHT OF FAITH

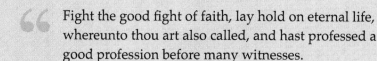

> Fight the good fight of faith, lay hold on eternal life,
> whereunto thou art also called, and hast professed a
> good profession before many witnesses.

1 TIMOTHY 6:12

POWER PRINCIPLE

Hold on to eternal life through unwavering faith and a bold
confession.

PROPHETIC PRAYER

Heavenly Father, strengthen me to fight the good fight of faith. Help
me lay hold of eternal life, knowing that I am called by Your grace and
have professed my faith before others. Grant me courage and persever-
ance as I face challenges, knowing that victory is assured through Your
power and promises. In Jesus' Name, Amen.

PREPARATION FOR WAR

What strategy has God revealed to you after reading today's message?

_____
_____
_____
_____
_____

What are the next steps you need to take?

_____
_____
_____
_____
_____

Journal your prayer to God in response to His Word.

_____
_____
_____
_____
_____

SCRIPTURE WRITING & REFLECTION

_____
_____
_____
_____
_____
_____
_____
_____
_____

DAY 7: CROSS YOUR JORDAN

 Cross over the Jordan into the land that I am giving to the children of Israel. I have given you every place where the sole of your foot will tread.

JOSHUA 1:2-3

POWER PRINCIPLE

God leads us to the inheritance He has prepared for us.

PROPHETIC PRAYER

Lord, like You spoke to Joshua after Moses' death, speak to me and guide me as I cross my Jordan into the land of promise. Help me to be strong and courageous, trusting in Your faithfulness and the assurance of the territories You have given. I declare that I will possess every place my feet tread upon, for You are with me. In Jesus' Name, Amen.

PREPARATION FOR WAR

What strategy has God revealed to you after reading today's message?

_____

_____

_____

_____

_____

What are the next steps you need to take?

_____

_____

_____

_____

_____

Journal your prayer to God in response to His Word.

_____

_____

_____

_____

_____

SCRIPTURE WRITING & REFLECTION

_____

_____

_____

_____

_____

_____

_____

_____

DAY 8: VIOLENTLY PURSUE THE KINGDOM OF HEAVEN

> And from the days of John the Baptist until now the kingdom of heaven suffereth violence, and the violent take it by force.

MATTHEW 11:12

POWER PRINCIPLE

With fervent determination, we pursue God's kingdom and seize its blessings.

PROPHETIC PRAYER

Lord, I understand that Your kingdom suffers violence, and I desire to passionately pursue You and Your kingdom. Help me to press forward with zeal, seeking Your will and aligning my life with Your purposes. Grant me the strength to overcome every obstacle, taking hold of the abundant life You have promised. In Jesus' Name, Amen.

PREPARATION FOR WAR

What strategy has God revealed to you after reading today's message?

_____

_____

_____

_____

_____

What are the next steps you need to take?

_____

_____

_____

_____

_____

Journal your prayer to God in response to His Word.

_____

_____

_____

_____

_____

SCRIPTURE WRITING & REFLECTION

_____

_____

_____

_____

_____

_____

_____

_____

DAY 9: WRESTLE THROUGH PRAYER

 And he said, I will not let thee go, except thou bless me.

GENESIS 32:26

POWER PRINCIPLE

In persistent prayer, we find strength and blessing from God.

PROPHETIC PRAYER

Heavenly Father, like Jacob who wrestled with You, I seek Your blessing and guidance in my life. Teach me the importance of persistent prayer and surrendering my desires to Your will. Even when facing challenges, I will not let go until You bless me. Strengthen me in the process, knowing that I have power with You and that I will prevail in Your grace. In Jesus' Name, Amen.

PREPARATION FOR WAR

What strategy has God revealed to you after reading today's message?

_____
_____
_____
_____
_____

What are the next steps you need to take?

_____
_____
_____
_____
_____

Journal your prayer to God in response to His Word.

_____
_____
_____
_____
_____

SCRIPTURE WRITING & REFLECTION

_____
_____
_____
_____
_____
_____
_____
_____

DAY 10: WITNESS HIS GREATNESS

> Even every one that is called by my name: for I have created him for my glory. I have declared, and have saved, and I have shewed, when there was no strange god among you: therefore ye are my witnesses, saith the Lord, that I am God.

ISAIAH 43:7,12

POWER PRINCIPLE

We are chosen by God to bear witness to His majesty and glory.

PROPHETIC PRAYER

O Lord, I am grateful that You have created me for Your glory. As a witness of Your greatness, help me to shine Your light and share Your truth with others. May my life be a living testimony to Your power, love, and salvation. Guide me to bring forth Your message to all nations and to lead others into a personal relationship with You. In Jesus' Name, Amen.

PREPARATION FOR WAR

What strategy has God revealed to you after reading today's message?

_____

_____

_____

_____

_____

What are the next steps you need to take?

_____

_____

_____

_____

_____

Journal your prayer to God in response to His Word.

_____

_____

_____

_____

_____

SCRIPTURE WRITING & REFLECTION

_____

_____

_____

_____

_____

_____

_____

_____

DAY 11: THE POTTER AND THE CLAY

> Arise, and go down to the potter's house, and there I will cause thee to hear my words. Then the word of the Lord came to me, saying, O house of Israel, cannot I do with you as this potter? Behold, as the clay is in the potter's hand, so are ye in mine hand, O house of Israel.

JEREMIAH 18: 2, 5-6

POWER PRINCIPLE

God shapes and molds us according to His divine plan.

PROPHETIC PRAYER

Heavenly Father, just as Jeremiah witnessed the potter molding the clay, I submit myself to Your divine craftsmanship. You are the Potter, and I am the clay. Mold me, shape me, and guide me according to Your perfect will. Help me to trust in Your loving hands, knowing that You will make me into a vessel that brings glory to Your name. In Jesus' Name, Amen.

PREPARATION FOR WAR

What strategy has God revealed to you after reading today's message?

_____
_____
_____
_____
_____

What are the next steps you need to take?

_____
_____
_____
_____
_____

Journal your prayer to God in response to His Word.

_____
_____
_____
_____
_____

SCRIPTURE WRITING & REFLECTION

_____
_____
_____
_____
_____
_____
_____
_____

DAY 12: BE CONFIDENT IN THE FACE OF ADVERSITY

> When the wicked, even mine enemies and my foes, came upon me to eat up my flesh, they stumbled and fell. Though an host should encamp against me, my heart shall not fear: though war should rise against me, in this will I be confident.
>
> PSALM 27:2-3

POWER PRINCIPLE

In God's strength, we face challenges with unwavering confidence.

PROPHETIC PRAYER

Lord, when enemies arise against me, I take refuge in You. You are my strength and my shield. Grant me the confidence to stand firm in the face of adversity, knowing that You are with me. I choose not to fear, for You are my deliverer. Empower me to trust in Your unfailing love and protection. In Jesus' Name, Amen.

PREPARATION FOR WAR

What strategy has God revealed to you after reading today's message?

_____

_____

_____

_____

_____

What are the next steps you need to take?

_____

_____

_____

_____

_____

Journal your prayer to God in response to His Word.

_____

_____

_____

_____

_____

SCRIPTURE WRITING & REFLECTION

_____

_____

_____

_____

_____

_____

_____

_____

DAY 13: SEEK GOD'S PRESENCE AND BLESSING

 Who shall ascend into the hill of the Lord? Or who shall stand in his holy place? He that hath clean hands, and a pure heart; who hath not lifted up his soul unto vanity, nor sworn deceitfully. He shall receive the blessing from the Lord.

PSALM 24:3-5

POWER PRINCIPLE

Those who seek God with a pure heart receive His blessing and righteousness.

PROPHETIC PRAYER

O Lord, the earth and all that dwells in it are Yours. Help me to seek Your face and stand in Your holy place. Cleanse my hands, purify my heart, and lead me in righteousness. I desire Your blessing and salvation in my life. This is the generation that seeks You, O God. May Your face shine upon us. In Jesus' Name, Amen.

PREPARATION FOR WAR

What strategy has God revealed to you after reading today's message?

_____

_____

_____

_____

_____

What are the next steps you need to take?

_____

_____

_____

_____

_____

Journal your prayer to God in response to His Word.

_____

_____

_____

_____

_____

SCRIPTURE WRITING & REFLECTION

_____

_____

_____

_____

_____

_____

_____

_____

DAY 14: FULFILL ALL RIGHTEOUSNESS THROUGH BAPTISM

> But John forbad him, saying, I have need to be baptized of thee, and comest thou to me? And Jesus answering said unto him, Suffer it to be so now: for thus it becometh us to fulfil all righteousness. Then he suffered him.
>
> MATTHEW 3:14-15

POWER PRINCIPLE

Obeying God's commandments leads to fulfilling His righteousness.

PROPHETIC PRAYER

Dear Lord, just as Jesus humbly obeyed and was baptized by John, help me to walk in obedience to Your Word and fulfill all righteousness. As I surrender to Your will, open the heavens above me and fill me with Your Holy Spirit. In Jesus' Name, Amen.

PREPARATION FOR WAR

What strategy has God revealed to you after reading today's message?

_____

_____

_____

_____

_____

What are the next steps you need to take?

_____

_____

_____

_____

_____

Journal your prayer to God in response to His Word.

_____

_____

_____

_____

_____

SCRIPTURE WRITING & REFLECTION

_____

_____

_____

_____

_____

_____

_____

_____

DAY 15: NO WEAPON SHALL PROSPER

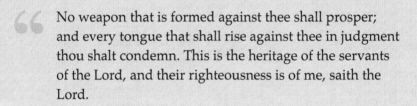

> No weapon that is formed against thee shall prosper; and every tongue that shall rise against thee in judgment thou shalt condemn. This is the heritage of the servants of the Lord, and their righteousness is of me, saith the Lord.

ISAIAH 54:17

POWER PRINCIPLE

God's protection prevails against every weapon formed against us.

PROPHETIC PRAYER

Mighty God, I take comfort in the promise that no weapon formed against me shall prosper. You have created me and granted me righteousness through Your Son, Jesus Christ. I rebuke every tongue that rises against me in judgment and trust in Your deliverance. Your heritage of protection is upon me. I rest in Your unfailing love and assurance. In Jesus' Name, Amen.

PREPARATION FOR WAR

What strategy has God revealed to you after reading today's message?

_____

_____

_____

_____

_____

What are the next steps you need to take?

_____

_____

_____

_____

_____

Journal your prayer to God in response to His Word.

_____

_____

_____

_____

_____

SCRIPTURE WRITING & REFLECTION

_____

_____

_____

_____

_____

_____

_____

_____

DAY 16: INVITATION TO THE WATERS OF LIFE

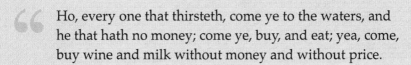

> Ho, every one that thirsteth, come ye to the waters, and he that hath no money; come ye, buy, and eat; yea, come, buy wine and milk without money and without price.

ISAIAH 55:1

POWER PRINCIPLE

God's invitation is open to all, offering spiritual abundance freely.

PROPHETIC PRAYER

Heavenly Father, thank You for the invitation to come to the waters of life. I come, not with money, but with a thirsty heart. Fill me with the wine and milk of Your grace. May I partake of the richness of Your love without price. In Jesus' Name, Amen.

PREPARATION FOR WAR

What strategy has God revealed to you after reading today's message?

_____
_____
_____
_____
_____

What are the next steps you need to take?

_____
_____
_____
_____
_____

Journal your prayer to God in response to His Word.

_____
_____
_____
_____
_____

SCRIPTURE WRITING & REFLECTION

_____
_____
_____
_____
_____
_____
_____
_____

DAY 17: BLESSED ARE THE HUNGRY AND THIRSTY

 Blessed are they which do hunger and thirst after righteousness: for they shall be filled.

MATTHEW 5:6

POWER PRINCIPLE

Those who hunger and thirst for righteousness will be filled.

PROPHETIC PRAYER

Lord, create in me a hunger and thirst for righteousness. May my soul
long for Your ways. I trust in Your promise that those who seek righteousness will be filled. Satisfy the deep longings of my heart with Your
goodness. In Jesus' Name, Amen.

PREPARATION FOR WAR

What strategy has God revealed to you after reading today's message?

_____

_____

_____

_____

_____

What are the next steps you need to take?

_____

_____

_____

_____

_____

Journal your prayer to God in response to His Word.

_____

_____

_____

_____

_____

SCRIPTURE WRITING & REFLECTION

_____

_____

_____

_____

_____

_____

_____

_____

DAY 18: JOYFUL JOURNEY WITH GOD

> For ye shall go out with joy, and be led forth with peace: the mountains and the hills shall break forth before you into singing, and all the trees of the field shall clap their hands. Instead of the thorn shall come up the fir tree, and instead of the brier shall come up the myrtle tree: and it shall be to the Lord for a name, for an everlasting sign that shall not be cut off.
>
> ISAIAH 55:12-13

POWER PRINCIPLE

Following God leads to joy, transformation, and everlasting signs.

PROPHETIC PRAYER

Dear God, lead me forth with joy, and let peace guide my steps. May the barren places in my life be transformed into places of growth and beauty. I trust in Your promises to make my way joyful and fruitful. In Jesus' Name, Amen.

PREPARATION FOR WAR

What strategy has God revealed to you after reading today's message?

_____

_____

_____

_____

_____

What are the next steps you need to take?

_____

_____

_____

_____

Journal your prayer to God in response to His Word.

_____

_____

_____

_____

SCRIPTURE WRITING & REFLECTION

_____

_____

_____

_____

_____

_____

_____

DAY 19: SEEK THE LORD AND HIS MERCY

> Seek ye the Lord while he may be found, call ye upon him while he is near: Let the wicked forsake his way, and the unrighteous man his thoughts: and let him return unto the Lord, and he will have mercy upon him; and to our God, for he will abundantly pardon.

ISAIAH 55:6-7

POWER PRINCIPLE

Seeking the Lord leads to an everlasting covenant and abundant pardon.

PROPHETIC PRAYER

Gracious God, I incline my ear to You, seeking Your presence. I hear Your call to return and repent. Thank You for the promise of an everlasting covenant and abundant pardon. Help me to forsake my ways and turn to You. In Jesus' Name, Amen.

PREPARATION FOR WAR

What strategy has God revealed to you after reading today's message?

_____

_____

_____

_____

_____

What are the next steps you need to take?

_____

_____

_____

_____

_____

Journal your prayer to God in response to His Word.

_____

_____

_____

_____

_____

SCRIPTURE WRITING & REFLECTION

_____

_____

_____

_____

_____

_____

_____

_____

DAY 20: BREAKING FORTH IN INHERITANCE

 For thou shalt break forth on the right hand and on the left; and thy seed shall inherit the Gentiles, and make the desolate cities to be inhabited. Fear not; for thou shalt not be ashamed: neither be thou confounded; for thou shalt not be put to shame: for thou shalt forget the shame of thy youth, and shalt not remember the reproach of thy widowhood any more.

ISAIAH 54:3–4

POWER PRINCIPLE

God breaks forth blessings, removing shame, and granting inheritance.

PROPHETIC PRAYER

Heavenly Father, I trust in Your promise to break forth blessings on every side. Remove shame and reproach from my life. Help me to fear not and inherit the abundant life You have prepared. May desolate places be inhabited by Your grace. In Jesus' Name, Amen.

PREPARATION FOR WAR

What strategy has God revealed to you after reading today's message?

_____
_____
_____
_____
_____

What are the next steps you need to take?

_____
_____
_____
_____
_____

Journal your prayer to God in response to His Word.

_____
_____
_____
_____
_____

SCRIPTURE WRITING & REFLECTION

_____
_____
_____
_____
_____
_____
_____
_____

DAY 21: A NEW THING - GOD'S PROMISE OF RENEWAL

> Remember ye not the former things, neither consider the things of old. Behold, I will do a new thing; now it shall spring forth; shall ye not know it? I will even make a way in the wilderness, and rivers in the desert.

ISAIAH 43:18–19

POWER PRINCIPLE

God promises to do a new thing and make a way in the wilderness.

PROPHETIC PRAYER

Heavenly Father, help me to release the past and embrace the new thing You are doing in my life. Make a way in my wilderness and bring forth rivers in my desert. I trust in Your promise of renewal. In Jesus' Name, Amen.

PREPARATION FOR WAR

What strategy has God revealed to you after reading today's message?

_____

_____

_____

_____

_____

What are the next steps you need to take?

_____

_____

_____

_____

_____

Journal your prayer to God in response to His Word.

_____

_____

_____

_____

_____

SCRIPTURE WRITING & REFLECTION

_____

_____

_____

_____

_____

_____

_____

_____

DAY 22: A NEW CREATURE IN CHRIST

 Therefore if any man be in Christ, he is a new creature: old things are passed away; behold, all things are become new.

2 CORINTHIANS 5:17

POWER PRINCIPLE

Being in Christ makes us new; old things pass away, and all things become new.

PROPHETIC PRAYER

Lord, thank You for making me a new creature in Christ. I surrender my old ways to embrace the newness that comes from being in You. Help me to live according to the truth that I am a new creation. In Jesus' Name, Amen.

PREPARATION FOR WAR

What strategy has God revealed to you after reading today's message?

_____
_____
_____
_____
_____

What are the next steps you need to take?

_____
_____
_____
_____
_____

Journal your prayer to God in response to His Word.

_____
_____
_____
_____
_____

SCRIPTURE WRITING & REFLECTION

_____
_____
_____
_____
_____
_____
_____
_____

DAY 23: ASSURED IN GOD'S LOVE

 He that spared not his own Son, but delivered him up
for us all, how shall he not with him also freely give us
all things?

ROMANS 8:32

POWER PRINCIPLE

God, who gave His Son, freely gives us all things and secures us in His
love.

PROPHETIC PRAYER

Heavenly Father, I stand in awe of Your love. Thank You for not
sparing Your Son, but delivering Him for us. I rest in the assurance that
nothing can separate me from Your love. In Jesus' Name, Amen.

PREPARATION FOR WAR

What strategy has God revealed to you after reading today's message?

_____

_____

_____

_____

_____

What are the next steps you need to take?

_____

_____

_____

_____

_____

Journal your prayer to God in response to His Word.

_____

_____

_____

_____

_____

SCRIPTURE WRITING & REFLECTION

_____

_____

_____

_____

_____

_____

_____

_____

DAY 24: CALLED AND SENT

 And the Lord looked upon him, and said, Go in this thy might, and thou shalt save Israel from the hand of the Midianites: have not I sent thee?

JUDGES 6:13-14

POWER PRINCIPLE

God calls and sends us, empowering us for the tasks He assigns.

PROPHETIC PRAYER

Lord, like Gideon, I may question Your presence in difficult times. Yet, I trust that You call and send me with Your strength. Help me to recognize Your guidance and respond with faith. In Jesus' Name, Amen.

PREPARATION FOR WAR

What strategy has God revealed to you after reading today's message?

_____

_____

_____

_____

_____

What are the next steps you need to take?

_____

_____

_____

_____

_____

Journal your prayer to God in response to His Word.

_____

_____

_____

_____

_____

SCRIPTURE WRITING & REFLECTION

_____

_____

_____

_____

_____

_____

_____

_____

DAY 25: THE LORD IS WITH THEE

 And the angel of the Lord appeared unto him, and said unto him, The Lord is with thee, thou mighty man of valour.

JUDGES 6:12

POWER PRINCIPLE

God sees us through His eyes of strength and potential.

PROPHETIC PRAYER

Gracious God, help me to see myself as You see me— a person of valor and strength. Thank You for affirming my identity in Christ. I trust that Your presence equips me for every task. In Jesus' Name, Amen.

PREPARATION FOR WAR

What strategy has God revealed to you after reading today's message?

_____

_____

_____

_____

_____

What are the next steps you need to take?

_____

_____

_____

_____

_____

Journal your prayer to God in response to His Word.

_____

_____

_____

_____

_____

SCRIPTURE WRITING & REFLECTION

_____

_____

_____

_____

_____

_____

_____

_____

DAY 26: ENDURE HARDNESS AS A GOOD SOLDIER

" Thou therefore endure hardness, as a good soldier of Jesus Christ. No man that warreth entangleth himself with the affairs of this life; that he may please him who hath chosen him to be a soldier.

2 TIMOTHY 2:3–4

POWER PRINCIPLE

Enduring hardships as a good soldier of Christ leads to pleasing Him.

PROPHETIC PRAYER

Lord, grant me the strength to endure hardships as a good soldier of Jesus Christ. Help me not to be entangled in worldly affairs, but to focus on pleasing You. In Jesus' Name, Amen.

PREPARATION FOR WAR

What strategy has God revealed to you after reading today's message?

_____
_____
_____
_____
_____

What are the next steps you need to take?

_____
_____
_____
_____
_____

Journal your prayer to God in response to His Word.

_____
_____
_____
_____
_____

SCRIPTURE WRITING & REFLECTION

_____
_____
_____
_____
_____
_____
_____
_____

DAY 27: THE WALL WILL FALL

> And it shall come to pass, that when they make a long blast with the ram's horn, and when ye hear the sound of the trumpet, all the people shall shout with a great shout; and the wall of the city shall fall down flat, and the people shall ascend up every man straight before him.

JOSHUA 6: 5-6, 12-13

POWER PRINCIPLE

With God as our Captain, we face battles with His guidance and strength.

PROPHETIC PRAYER

Heavenly Captain, guide me in the battles I face. Help me to recognize Your authority and submit to Your leading. Grant me the courage to follow You into victory. In Jesus' Name, Amen.

PREPARATION FOR WAR

What strategy has God revealed to you after reading today's message?

_____
_____
_____
_____
_____

What are the next steps you need to take?

_____
_____
_____
_____
_____

Journal your prayer to God in response to His Word.

_____
_____
_____
_____
_____

SCRIPTURE WRITING & REFLECTION

_____
_____
_____
_____
_____
_____
_____
_____

DAY 28: LORD OF WAR

 The Lord is a man of war: the Lord is his name.

EXODUS 15:3

POWER PRINCIPLE

In the Lord, we find strength and victory in spiritual battles.

PROPHETIC PRAYER

Lord, You are a warrior who fights for us. I take refuge in Your strength and trust in Your victory. Help me to stand firm in spiritual battles, knowing that You are with me. In Jesus' Name, Amen.

PREPARATION FOR WAR

What strategy has God revealed to you after reading today's message?

_____

_____

_____

_____

_____

What are the next steps you need to take?

_____

_____

_____

_____

_____

Journal your prayer to God in response to His Word.

_____

_____

_____

_____

_____

SCRIPTURE WRITING & REFLECTION

_____

_____

_____

_____

_____

_____

_____

_____

DAY 29: GIDEON'S CALL AND ASSURANCE

> Then the Lord turned to him and said, 'Go in this might of yours, and you shall save Israel from the hand of the Midianites. Have I not sent you?' And the Lord said to him, 'Surely I will be with you, and you shall defeat the Midianites as one man.'

JUDGES 6: 14, 16

POWER PRINCIPLE

God's call is accompanied by His presence and assurance.

PROPHETIC PRAYER

Lord, as You called and assured Gideon, I trust in Your calling on my life. May Your presence and assurance empower me to fulfill the tasks You assign. In Jesus' Name, Amen.

PREPARATION FOR WAR

What strategy has God revealed to you after reading today's message?

_____

_____

_____

_____

_____

What are the next steps you need to take?

_____

_____

_____

_____

_____

Journal your prayer to God in response to His Word.

_____

_____

_____

_____

_____

SCRIPTURE WRITING & REFLECTION

_____

_____

_____

_____

_____

_____

_____

_____

DAY 30: DECREEING AND ESTABLISHING

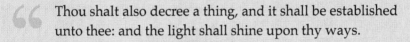

Thou shalt also decree a thing, and it shall be established unto thee: and the light shall shine upon thy ways.

JOB 22:28

POWER PRINCIPLE

Our words have power; decreeing aligns us with God's purpose.

PROPHETIC PRAYER

Lord, I declare Your promises over my life. As I decree according to Your will, may it be established unto me. Let Your light shine upon my ways. In Jesus' Name, Amen.

PREPARATION FOR WAR

What strategy has God revealed to you after reading today's message?

_____

_____

_____

_____

_____

What are the next steps you need to take?

_____

_____

_____

_____

_____

Journal your prayer to God in response to His Word.

_____

_____

_____

_____

_____

SCRIPTURE WRITING & REFLECTION

_____

_____

_____

_____

_____

_____

_____

_____

ABOUT THE AUTHOR

Apostle Gary M. Dunn, Sr. serves as the senior pastor of End Time Harvest Global Ministries in Baltimore, Maryland. Born and raised in Baltimore, he responded to the divine call of the Lord Jesus Christ to ministry in 1980. Since then, he has dedicated his life to serving the Lord and His people with joy and passion.

Throughout his ministry journey, Apostle Dunn has served in various capacities, including tent (outreach) ministry, youth and children's ministry, marriage ministry, prison ministry, women's ministry, and mentoring men. Recognized as a vital part of the five-fold ministry, he has been called as an Apostle to equip new converts and train leadership for the work of the ministry. His vision is centered on fostering unity within the Body of Christ, nurturing growth in maturity and faith, and deepening knowledge of Jesus Christ, as outlined in Ephesians 4:3-16.

Additionally, Apostle Dunn has received the Apostleship of the Holy Ghost to spearhead church planting efforts and expand the reach of the Gospel globally, particularly in Asia and Africa. He is known as an "end-time globalist," dedicated to spreading the message of Jesus Christ to the nations. Apostle Dunn mentors and fathers other apostles, pastors, and evangelists, nurturing their growth and development in ministry.

At the core of Apostle Dunn's heart is Isaiah 61:1-3, embodying his passion for setting souls free, healing the brokenhearted, and delivering those in need. He is a loving father to his sons James S. Dunn, Gary M. Dunn, Jr., Collie I. Dunn, and Timothy L. Dunn, Sr. He is a proud grandfather to Timothy Jr., Julius, Shamal, and Jaleea. Apostle Dunn considers himself a spiritual father to many sons and daughters of Jesus Christ, guiding them in their spiritual journey with wisdom and love.

To get in touch with Apostle Gary Dunn, please contact him here:
Email: mdunn5757@gmail.com

Made in the USA
Columbia, SC
28 April 2025

57210159R00041